Thanks, Aunt Zelda!

Thank-You Cards for Kids to Craft

by

Cynthia MacGregor

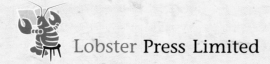

Lobster Press Limited

MacGregor, Cynthia, 1943–
Thanks, Aunt Zelda!
Text © 2002 Cynthia MacGregor
Illustrations © 2002 Anouk Pérusse-Bell

Published by Lobster Press™
1620 Sherbrooke Street West, Suites C & D
Montréal, Québec   H3H 1C9
Tel. (514) 904-1100 · Fax (514) 904-1101 · www.lobsterpress.com

Publisher: Alison Fripp
Editor: Julie Mahfood
Design & layout: Zack Taylor Design

Distributed in the United States by:
Publishers Group West
1700 Fourth Street
Berkeley, CA 94710

Distributed in Canada by:
Raincoast Books
9050 Shaughnessey Street
Vancouver, BC V6P 6E5

We acknowledge the financial support of the Government of Canada through the Book Publishing Industry Development Program (BPIDP) for our publishing activities.

Canada Council **Conseil des Arts**
for the Arts **du Canada**

We acknowledge the support of the Canada Council for the Arts for our publishing program.

National Library of Canada Cataloguing in Publication

MacGregor, Cynthia
    Thanks, Aunt Zelda! : thank-you cards for kids to craft Cynthia MacGregor ; Anouk Pérusse-Bell, illustrator.

ISBN 1-894222-66-0

    1. Greeting cards—Juvenile literature.   2. Thank-you notes—Juvenile literature.
I. Pérusse Bell, Anouk II. Title.

TT872.M33 2002   J745.594'1   C2002-901412-3

Printed in Hong Kong, China

Dedication

For Justin, Tori, Steffan, and Aiden

Contents

For Jigsaw Note craft, please see page 33.

Chapter 1

Everyone Loves to Get Presents!

If you asked most kids what the best

part is about having a birthday, what do you think they would answer? (What would *you* answer?)

It isn't the fact that it's your special day, and everyone makes a fuss over you. Certainly almost everybody likes that. But that's not the *best* part, is it? It isn't the fact that you get to be one year older, although that's pretty cool, too. Right?

It isn't the party. Sure, parties are lots of fun. Whether you play games at home, go to a video game arcade, go bowling, have a pizza party, or do some other special fun thing, nearly everyone loves to have a birthday party. Being surrounded by your friends, who all wish you "Happy Birthday!" is great. Eating a big, gooey layer cake with your favorite icing is something you don't get to do every day, either. Still, that's not the best part of having a birthday...at least, not for most kids. But now that we're talking about the party, we're getting closer.

It's what everyone *brings* to the party. That's the best part, isn't it? The presents! The best part of birthdays (and other gift-giving occasions, like Christmas and Chanukah), for most kids, is getting all those presents: presents from your family, presents from your friends. Presents from your Great-Aunt Myra in Peoria and your Grandpa Ted in Toronto. Lots and lots of presents.

But there's a downside to getting presents, isn't there? Yes, I'm talking about *The Dreaded Thank-You Note*.

"Awwww, Mommmmm! Do I really hafta write a thank-you?" Does this sound like you? Sure, like you and every other kid. But yes, you really do have to write a thank-you note.

Since you have to anyway (and I'm going to tell you why you do), this book is here to help. You can learn to write a thank-you that is almost painless. In fact, I'm going to show you how to create thank-you letters and cards that can actually be (are you ready for this?) *fun* to make!

I'll tell you about making the letters and cards later. (I'm saving the best for last.) First, let's talk about writing thank-you notes. Ready?

Chapter 2

Are Thank-You Notes Really Necessary?

Why do you have to write thank-you

notes for presents? (I bet you've asked your mom or dad the same question...and more than once!) Well, there are a number of reasons.

Most importantly, it shows that you're really appreciative. Let's say you got a new video game from your Aunt Kim for Christmas. Did your aunt just run out to the store and buy you the first thing she saw? Nope! If she did, you might have gotten a package of prunes, a sweatshirt with the logo of some hockey team you don't even like, or a pink-striped pencil case.

But that's not what she gave you. (Whew!)

She gave you a video game. One that you don't already have. One that you *like*. Cool gift, huh? Does she know how much you like it? Does she know how perfect her present was?

Your Aunt Kim probably went to a bunch of different stores, looking for the perfect gift for you, before she thought of a video game. Or maybe she sat at home, thinking and thinking and thinking about what to get you for Christmas, and finally she thought of getting you a video game. Maybe she called your mom to double check and make sure that you didn't already have that one. Maybe she had to phone a number of stores before she found one with the right game.

In other words, buying your gift wasn't something she did quickly. It took time. (It took money, too. Video games aren't cheap!) She deserves a big "Thank you!" for doing that—more than a quick word or two when she hands it to you or a few words by phone if she lives far away.

You see, one thing about thank-you notes is that when you take the time to sit down and write a short letter thanking someone for a present, you show them that you appreciate what they did. They took the time and made the effort to get you the best gift they could think of. You, in turn, need to make the time and effort to write them a note of thanks.

Even if you don't like the gift, it's still good manners to thank the person for giving it to you (and in another chapter we'll talk about writing notes for gifts you hate). After all, they didn't *intentionally* give you a gift they knew you'd hate. They just guessed wrong. You can appreciate the gift—and the fact that the giver meant well, and the fact that he or she went to some trouble and spent some money. You can *appreciate* something even if you don't *like* it.

It's a matter of manners, just like saying "Please" and "Excuse me" and covering your mouth when you yawn or your nose when you sneeze.

Nobody *likes* writing thank-you notes. Not me—not even your mom. But we all do it. You have to, too.

Of course, not *every* gift requires a thank-you note. You don't have to write one for presents from your parents, or from your sister or brother who lives with you. (If your sister is away at college, though, it might be nice to send a note or at least an email to thank her for the present she sent.) If it's from your grandma or grandpa who lives nearby, or someone you see often, your mom might excuse you from writing a thank-you note. And not all parents agree about presents you get at a party. Some parents feel it's necessary to write thank-you notes for these gifts, but some feel it's okay to skip it and just thank your friends out loud.

But most any other present calls for a thank-you note.

When the present arrives by mail (or some other delivery service like FedEx or UPS), it's even more important. Now you not only need to tell the person that you appreciate the present, you also need to tell them that you got it in the first place. Packages do get lost in the mail once in a while. Did a friend of your dad's send you a sweater? Did your aunt send you a book? He or she will want to know that it arrived safely.

And of course, while you're letting the giver know you got the gift, you will thank them for it. (And if you think the gift is just great, by all means say so!)

So stop trying to fudge your way out of it. Write that note!

Chapter 3

I Said 'Thank You'— Now What?

Yes, I know. It's not easy. When you're talking to someone in person—let's say it's Aunt Liz—you can say, "Thanks for the CD. That's my favorite group!"

Aunt Liz will immediately say, "You're welcome. I hope you enjoy it." And then she'll ask you about school, or you can ask her how your cousin Jeff is, and you're on to talking about other things.

It seems much easier, doesn't it?

But you know what? Thank-you notes can be almost that easy.

How do you write a thank-you note? We're going to write one together. You start with the *salutation*:

Dear Aunt Liz,

(There. That wasn't so difficult, was it? You'll be surprised how easy the rest of it can be, too!)

Next, you can add something polite like you might say at the start of any conversation (except you won't have Aunt Liz answering you back, so you have to make all the conversation yourself):

> How are you? How are Uncle Tom, and Jeff and Kari? I am fine.

Now, add a little bit of news or chit-chat:

> School is good this year. Classes are tough, but I am doing okay. I have a really tough teacher, but she is fair. My best friend is in my class, which is great. I am in the school band this year. I am learning to play the trombone!

If Aunt Liz already knows these things, you can find other stuff to tell her. There's certainly *some* news, something you've done recently that she doesn't know. Since you've gotten a present from her, you've probably either had a birthday or just celebrated Christmas or Chanukah, your elementary school graduation, a confirmation or bar mitzvah, or some other special occasion. Tell her a little about how the occasion was.

Now that you've taken care of giving her a little news (and used up some of that terrible blank space on the page!), you can get down to the *real* purpose of this letter—thanking her for her present. If you've just told her about your birthday party, or what you did on Christmas, you've given yourself a natural lead-in to talking about the present:

> I got a lot of presents for my birthday, but one of the best was the book you sent!

If that isn't true, you can still say:

> And, since I'm talking about my birthday, the reason I'm writing is to thank you for the book.

Now, you have to say *something* more than just "Thank you." Assuming you liked the present at all, you can find one or more nice things to say about it.

I've been wanting to read that book for a long time.

or

I borrowed that book from the library and loved it. It's so great to have a copy of my own now. I know I'll want to read it again and again.

That's my favorite rock group. The CD was a perfect gift! I know it may not be your kind of music, but it's my absolutely favorite!

The sweatshirt is exactly the right size, and of course I'm a Steelers fan, so that makes it perfect! Thank you for choosing just the right present.

That's one board game I don't have yet, and it looks like lots of fun. The next time one of my friends is over, we'll have to try it. It'll be fun to play a new game!

The badminton set looks like lots of fun. I played badminton in camp last summer. Mom is going to set up the net in the backyard for me. I bet I can get lots of practice and be great at the game by the time I go back to camp next summer!

Do you get the idea now? Certainly, the more nice things you can say about the present, the better it is. But if you write two or three sentences in which you compliment the gift, that's good enough.

What next?

You need some kind of sentence that sounds like an end to a conversation. If there is anything else you want to say, such as, "I hope you and Uncle Tom and Jeff and Kari will come and visit us soon," or "I hope you had a great Christmas, too," this would be a good place to say it. Otherwise, you can just say, "Well, thanks again for a really nice present," or some words like that. Then sign the letter with "Love," or "Sincerely," (depending on whom you're writing to) and sign your name.

See? You're finished!

Okay, it wasn't exactly fun, but that wasn't really so awful, was it? It's kind of like talking to someone. Just pretend you're on the phone, or talking face-to-face with Aunt Liz or Dad's friend Mr. Witherspoon, and say what you would say to her or him. Ask how he or she is feeling. Thank him or her for the present. Find something else to talk about for a minute. And then say "Goodbye" (which, in a letter, is done by signing it). And you're finished!

Chapter 4

"But I Hated the Present!"

What if you didn't like the present?

It happens. Unfortunately, it happens all too often. Maybe your goofy Uncle Ernie sent you a pair of lemon-yellow pants that you wouldn't give to your worst enemy. Maybe your Grandma Michelle knitted you a sweater…but it's the color of dog barf, and the neck is so big you could fit your head *and* your best friend's head through it at the same time.

Or maybe it's a near miss—a present that should have been great but isn't. Maybe your Grandma Ruth gave you a great video game…but it doesn't work on your video game system. Maybe Cousin Sue gave you a wool sweater that looks just super—but you're allergic to wool. Maybe your mom's friend Edith gave you a wonderful book…that you already have two copies of.

Now what are you going to write? How do you thank someone for gifts like those awful lemon-yellow pants…or that sweater you'll never be able to wear? Do you write and say, "I love it," when your mom is always reminding you how important it is to tell the truth?

Believe it or not, you can thank someone for a gift you hate—or like but can't use—without lying *or* telling the whole truth. It's all in what you say… and what you leave out!

You begin the thank-you note the usual way, with "Dear Uncle Ernie" (or whoever you're writing to). You go on from there with "How are you? I am fine," or some other pleasant bit of chit-chat. And then you have to thank him for the gift.

You may not feel like thanking him. The gift is ***awful***! You'll never wear those horrible pants. But remember this: You aren't just thanking him for the pants themselves. You're thanking him for thinking of you. You're thanking him for remembering your birthday, and for putting some thought into what to give you (even if he did guess spectacularly wrong!). You're thanking him for taking the time to go shopping, for spending money on you, and maybe even for going to the post office and standing in line to mail the package.

Remember what I said before: You may not *like* the gift; you can still *appreciate* it.

If the gift was handmade, rather than store-bought, the materials it was made out of still cost money, and the giver spent time on creating it. So don't think hand-made gifts need any less thanks than store-bought ones, just because "she made it herself." In fact, that's a very good reason for being *extra*-appreciative: *she made it herself*…just for you!

So…what are you going to write to your uncle, your grandma, your mom or dad's friend? How are you going to thank someone for a present you really hated? You know what you'd *like* to write! If you were allowed to be totally honest, you'd write:

Dear Grandma,

Where did you find a sweater exactly the color of dog barf? Well, one good thing—if Rusty ever throws up on it, no one will ever know the difference! It even has funny lumps that look like dog barf, too.

I'm glad you didn't send me a little-kids'-size sweater, like last year. But did you think I am fully grown already? I doubt I will ever be big enough to fit that sweater.

The neck is way too large. In winter, all the cold air can rush right in the opening.

And since the style doesn't look like anything any of my friends would ever wear, I would look like a total loser if I ever wore it.

But still, it was nice of you to remember me.

Love,

Lee

No, you can't write that note. Instead, find something good to say about the present. And, strangely enough, a good place to start is with some of the things you *don't* like about it. What's *good* about what you don't like?

→ The neck is too large? You can say it will never feel tight enough to choke you because it's good and loose. (No lie—it's the truth!)

→ The sweater's way too large? You can say you won't grow out of it for a long time. (That's the truth too. Even if you never wear it, it *won't ever* be too small for you.)

→ The color is blah? You can say it's a nice neutral color that will go with things in your wardrobe. (You're not actually promising to *wear* it with any of those things...or at all. But it *will* go with them.)

→ It doesn't look like anything you'd ever buy for yourself? You can say it's different from anything in your closet or dresser. (That's certainly true!)

Did someone give you perfume you like the smell of, but it makes you sneeze? Sometimes, you have to thank someone for a gift you like but can't use...for instance, a gift you're allergic to. In that case, you can be a little more honest— you're not saying you didn't like the gift, after all. This means you can tell Aunt Zelda of your inability to use it, and in that way prevent her from sending you the same thing next year.

You can write something like, "I really loved the smell of that fragrance. Wouldn't you know I'd have the rotten luck to be allergic to it! Gee, I wish I could wear it!" Or "That sweater is so warm and cozy, and it's absolutely gorgeous! I wish I weren't allergic to wool—it would be the perfect thing to wear this winter."

Did someone give you a book you love but already have? Say that the writer who wrote it is one of your favorite authors, or that you love the way he or she writes, or that you've read the book before and really love it and you're glad to own a copy. (Think about it—you haven't told a lie! You *do* love the book and you *are* glad to own a copy—the copy you already own. And now you can exchange *this* copy at the bookstore for something else you *really* want...and isn't that a good thing, too?!) Did someone give you a CD of a group you hate? Tell them they've managed to find a CD you don't already have. (Again, it's the truth!)

Instead you can write something like this:

Dear Grandma,

Thank you for the sweater. It is different from anything I already had in my dresser. I like having lots of different clothes.

The color is a good neutral. It will go with almost anything in my closet. The size is nice and large. I can keep that sweater for a while without worrying about outgrowing it. And the neck is nice and large, too. This is one sweater that will never give me that awful choking feeling.

Thanks again for thinking of me.

Love,

Lee

Now do you have the hang of it?

Here are just a few more suggestions for complimentary things you can honestly say about gifts you wish you hadn't gotten:

⇒ It matches my hair/eyes/favorite shirt/best friend's jacket.

⇒ It's just like Mom's/Dad's/my best friend's.

⇒ How did you know we have to read that book for school?!

⇒ It's a very useful present.

⇒ I can tell you worked hard to make me that present.

⇒ It looks nice and warm/strong/soft/sturdy.

⇒ It has nice, deep pockets—my keys and stuff won't fall out of *those* pants!

⇒ It's a very cheery color!

Now you try it! You don't have to actually write a note—just think up some things you could say if you got that pair of lemon-yellow pants, or a board game you once played at your best friend's house and hated, or an ugly shirt that's two sizes too small for you.

Chapter 5

Having Fun with Thank-Yous— Some Craft ideas

Of course, nobody says thank-you notes

have to always be the same ordinary letter written on ordinary stationery; there are plenty of ways to make thank-you notes more interesting! It can actually be *fun* to write a thank-you note, if you get clever and creative with the stationery...or with the note itself. You're about to read some ideas for thank-you notes you can *craft*, instead of just writing plain old notes. When you've picked a craft you like, read all the way through the directions once, before you start actually making it:

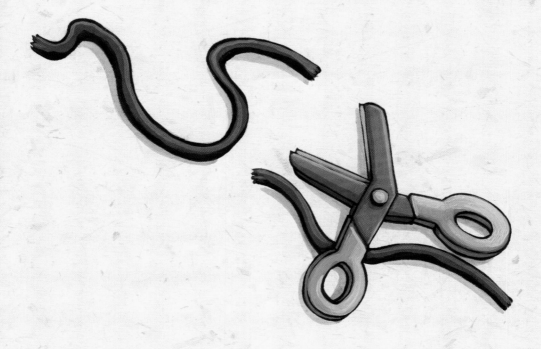

Collage Card

MATERIALS NEEDED One piece of reasonably heavy paper (computer paper or construction paper, or even light card stock); scissors; glue; a magazine your mom or dad doesn't want anymore that has pictures in it

PROCEDURE

1 Fold the piece of paper in half and turn it sideways so the fold is to your left. (It will now open like a standard greeting card.)

2 Cut out some pictures from the magazine.

  Note: If you're interested in sports, these might all be pictures from the world of sports. If you're interested in pets, they might all be images of cats, dogs, and horses. If it's around Christmas time, they might all be holiday pictures—holly, Christmas trees, poinsettia plants, Santa, reindeer, or a family gathered around a table. (You can also do this with any other holiday, such as Chanukah.) If the card is a thank-you for a springtime birthday, you might find a lot of pictures of flowers in a magazine. (The pictures don't *have* to all be on one theme, but it's generally better.)

  Cut around each picture so that you eliminate the background.

3 Glue the pictures onto the front of the card you are creating. Start with the biggest pictures first, and work down to the smaller ones. This way, you will fill the card up faster. As you may already know, a collage involves pictures overlapping each other, so part of one picture will hide part of another. The art in creating a collage is to do it in an attractive way, so it doesn't look like you just pasted the pictures down any old way on the card. When you are finished, there should be little or none of the white paper or card stock showing.

4 Now open the card you have created and write your thank-you message inside in the usual way.

Comic Character Note

MATERIALS NEEDED   One piece of computer paper; two or three small pictures of a comic book or comic strip character; scissors; glue; pen

PROCEDURE

1 Cut out two or three small pictures of a comic book or comic strip character. (It is preferable to cut right around the person or animal and leave out the background, but unlike the collage, above, it is not absolutely necessary.)

2 Glue characters on one side of the piece of paper, spaced apart from each other. If you've cut out two pictures, glue one at the top, the other in the middle. If you've cut out three, glue one at the top, one in the middle and one at the bottom. (Don't worry if it's not exact!) Don't glue them in the center of the page—glue them off to the left or right. This way, you will leave space for what the characters will "say."

3 Near to each comic character's face, write a short message...as if the character is saying it. Bonus points if you can make it sound like something the character *would* say, or tie it in to the character in some other way. For instance, if you have chosen a superhero: "It certainly was a SUPER present that you gave Lee for Christmas. Lee really wants to thank you for the new sneakers. How did you know exactly the right ones to get?" or "We heroes know how important it is to look cool, and you're Lee's hero for buying that totally cool jacket with the Dolphins logo on it!"

For a comic book cat, you can always write something like, "That was a PURR-fect gift you gave Lee."

The reason you have glued two or three pictures of the comic character is so that you can write two or three different things. (Of course, they don't all have to be about the gift. One can be the usual "I hope you're well" part of the note.)

4 Draw a comic book dialogue "balloon" around what you have written, with the point toward the character's mouth, as if he or she is speaking.

5 Sign your name at the bottom.

Glittering Stars Card

MATERIALS NEEDED   Light blue construction paper; dark blue construction paper; silver glitter; glue; aluminum foil; scissors

PROCEDURE

1 Fold the light blue construction paper over from top to bottom and turn it sideways so the fold is on your left. (This way it will open like a standard greeting card.)

2 Cut out a rectangle from the dark blue construction paper that is smaller than the front of your light blue card. It should be small enough that when placed in the middle of the front of the card, it leaves a one-inch border of light blue around the edges of the card. (One inch is approximate—it doesn't have to be exact.)

3 Glue the darker rectangle in the middle of the card. You now have a light blue border around a dark blue rectangle.

4 Lay down a thick line of glue all along the four edges of the darker rectangle. This line should overlap the edges of both colors of blue. Now, sprinkle glitter onto the glue. You will have a rectangular border of glitter which joins the dark paper to the light.

5 Tear off a length of aluminum foil perhaps five inches long. (It doesn't have to be exact!) Fold it over so that the shiny side is facing out. (Folding it will make it thicker and less likely to tear while you're cutting it.)

6 Cut out a crescent moon and a few stars from the aluminum foil. Make them an appropriate size for the card.

7 Glue them on the dark blue rectangle.

8 If you want, add a little silver glitter near the stars.

9 When the glue on the card is dry, open the card and write your thank-you message inside.

Jigsaw Note

MATERIALS NEEDED   One piece of heavy paper, such as construction paper (you want paper that will not be too difficult to cut, yet will not get bent easily); scissors; pen; pencil with eraser

PROCEDURE

1 Using a pen, write your thank-you note in the ordinary way.

2 Turn the sheet of paper over.

3 With a pencil, working on the back of the page, draw some lines that look like the cuts of a jigsaw puzzle. Draw lightly. If you're not happy with what you're drawing, erase it and draw again. Don't make it too complicated. You don't want the person you're sending the note to, to give up and never put the note together and read it. Probably cutting the note into between eight and fifteen pieces is good.

4 When you're happy with what you've drawn, cut along the lines. You have turned your thank-you note into a jigsaw puzzle, and the person you're sending it to will have to put it together in order to read it!

* For illustration of Jigsaw Note, please see page 6.

Yarn Picture Card

MATERIALS NEEDED   One piece of light-colored heavy paper (such as construction paper) or card stock; pencil; crayons or colored felt-tip pens; squeeze bottle of white glue with applicator tip; colored yarn; scissors

PROCEDURE

1 Fold the paper or card stock over from top to bottom and turn it sideways so the fold is on your left. (This way it will open like a standard greeting card.)

2 Using a pencil, draw a picture or a design on the front. Draw the outlines of a picture of your choice, a face, flower, animal, tree, moon, stars, or whatever. (It doesn't actually have to be a picture of something—it can just be a pretty design.) Next, go over your pencil-lines with colored pencils or crayons, to outline with the colors of yarn you'd like to use.

3 Use crayon (or felt-tip colored marker) to color in the area within the outlines. For example, if you drew a tulip and outlined it in red, you can cover the area within the outline with red crayon or marker.

4 With a squeeze-type bottle of white glue, carefully put down a line of glue over the outline of the picture. Just do one outline at a time, and work from the inside of the picture out. If, for example, you have a picture of a person, and you have drawn the outline of his body as well as his eyes, nose, and mouth, first do one eye, then the other, then the nose, the mouth, and finally the outline of his head, body, arms and legs.

5 When you have put down the glue line, cover the glue with a length of yarn the color of the crayon on the outline. Follow the outline carefully, all the way around. Snip the yarn when you reach the end.

6 Now open the card and write your thank-you note inside.

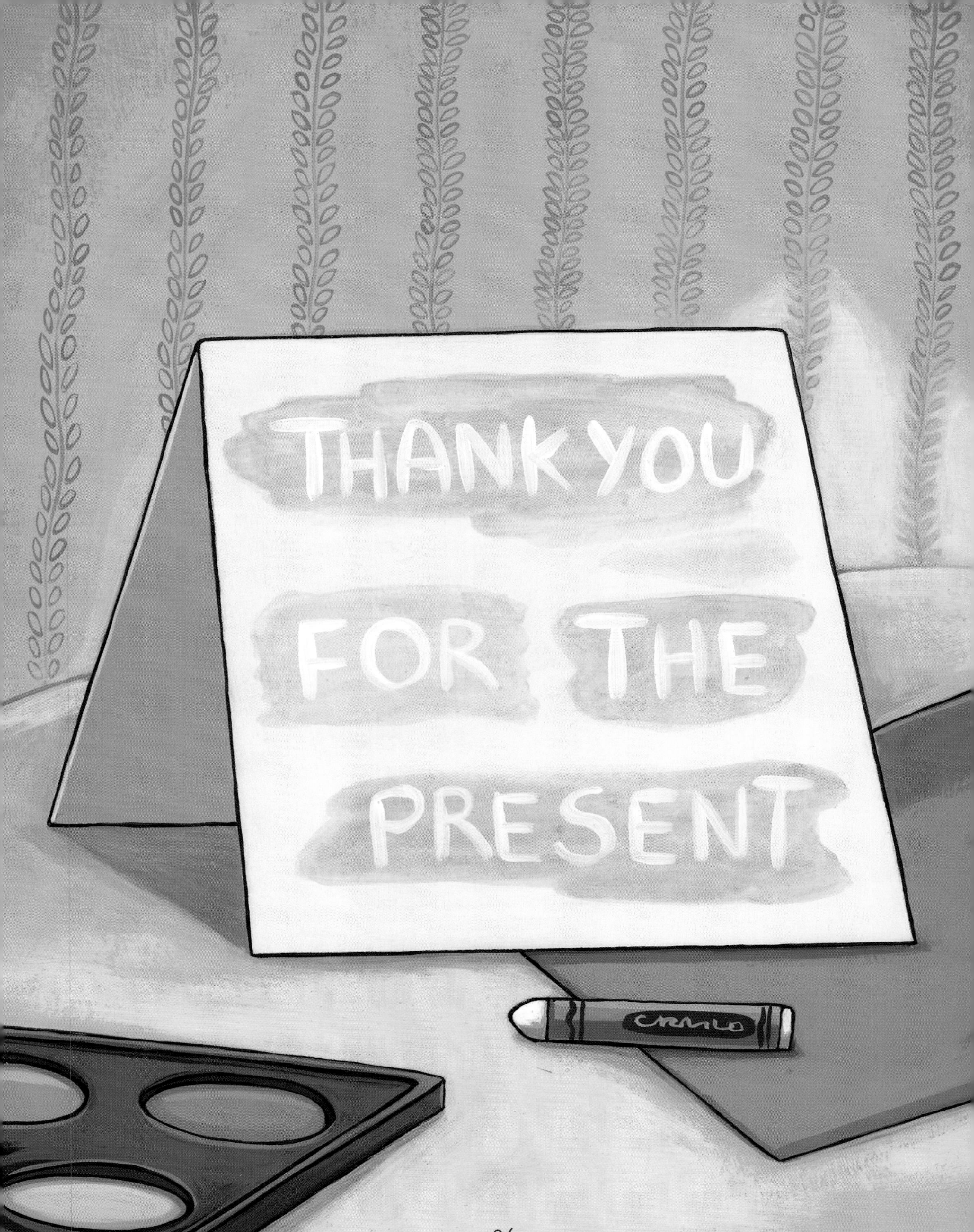
THANK YOU
FOR THE
PRESENT

White-on-White Card

MATERIALS NEEDED White construction paper, card stock or other reasonably heavy paper; white crayon; watercolor paints (preferably two or three different colors)

PROCEDURE

1 Fold the paper or card stock over from top to bottom and turn it sideways so the fold is on your left. (This way it will open like a standard greeting card.)

2 Write *THANK YOU* in big letters on the front of the white paper, using white crayon. (You will not be able to see it well, if at all.) Instead of simply *THANK YOU*, you may choose to write *THANK YOU FOR THE PRESENT*, or *A BIG "THANK YOU!"* or some similar words.

3 Using watercolors, paint across the words. (To help you find the letters on the card, so you know where to paint, run your finger lightly across the front of the card. You'll be able to *feel* the waxy crayon.) Do not cover the entire card with paint. Let some of the white paper show, but be sure to cover the entire message. Your *THANK YOU* message (in white crayon) will show through the paint. Now you (and the person you're sending the card to) will be able to read it.

   Note: If you've written more than just *THANK YOU*, try using two colors. Even if you write just *THANK YOU* and nothing more, try writing *THANK* very large on one line and *YOU* very large below it. Paint across *THANK* with one color of watercolors and across *YOU* with another.

4 Write your thank-you note inside.

Confetti Card

MATERIALS NEEDED One sheet of bright pastel construction paper (yellow is a good choice, but light blue or pink would work too); two or three other sheets of construction paper in different colors (these should contrast well with the first sheet); scissors; glue

PROCEDURE

1 Fold the paper that you are going to use as a card from top to bottom, and turn it sideways, so the fold is on your left. (This way it will open like a standard greeting card.)

2 Cut little pieces out of the other colors of paper. A good size is 1/4" x 3/4", though they don't have to be exact, and they don't have to all be exactly the same size.

3 Place the pieces on the front of the card. Arrange them in a pleasing pattern. The colors should be intermixed, with the pieces of paper not at regular intervals from each other or in any regular arrangement as far as the colors are concerned. They shouldn't all be straight up-and-down, either; some of them should be at different angles. It should look very random, like falling confetti. You can even overlap one piece over another in a few cases. *(**Hint:** Don't use too many pieces of paper; the finished card will look more attractive if there is a lot of yellow (or whatever color) background showing.)*

4 When you are happy with the arrangement, pick up one small piece of paper at a time and put glue on the back of it, then return it to its place and press down, gluing it in place. Don't use too much glue; you don't want the glue oozing out from the sides.

5 When the glue has dried and the front of the card is finished, open it up and write your thank-you note inside.

Shape Card

MATERIALS NEEDED One piece of reasonably heavy paper (computer paper or construction paper, or even light card stock); scissors; pencil; eraser; crayons *or* colored markers; pen; (optional: a picture cut from a magazine your mom or dad doesn't want anymore, which you can trace around to get the shape you need)

PROCEDURE

1 Fold the piece of paper in half. If the shape you're drawing is wider than it is long, you can experiment with which way your card will face, so that it best suits your needs. Maybe your card will have to open from top to bottom! Turn the card so that whichever way it faces, it will be a good fit for the shape you choose.

2 Decide what shape you want your card to be. (Some examples are a star, moon, dog, cat, fish, circle, house, person, heart, boat, rocket—but it doesn't have to be one of those. If the thank-you is for a birthday gift, you might want the shape of a birthday cake. For Christmas, you might want a Santa or a Christmas tree. It isn't necessary, though, for the picture to be something that has to do with the occasion.)

Decide whether you can draw the shape you want on your own. If you can't, look in a magazine for a picture you can trace of the object you want your card to be shaped like. (***Hint:*** *Be sure the picture is no bigger than your card.*)

3 If you have decided to trace a picture from a magazine, first cut out the picture from the magazine and then lay it down on the folded paper. (***Hint:*** *Be sure the fold is where you want it. Also be sure the picture lies right along the fold, so that you don't end up with two separate pieces of paper instead of one card with a fold joining the front and back.*)

4 Using a pencil, trace the magazine picture or draw the object you want the card to be shaped like. (*Hint: If you are drawing without tracing, you still need to be sure that the edge of the picture is right up against the fold.*)

5 Look at the picture after you have drawn or traced it, and make sure you are happy with it. Using the eraser and pencil, fix anything you don't like, until you are happy with the outline.

6 Now cut along the pencil lines, so you are left with a card the shape of whatever you chose. (*Hint: Don't cut the parts of the picture that are on the fold. If you do, you will cut the fold and separate the front of the card from the back. You want to make sure the two pieces stay attached.*)

7 If you used computer paper, you can erase any pencil lines that remain on the card. (*Hint: If you use an eraser on colored construction paper, the eraser can remove color from the paper. Instead of erasing, you can color your pencil outline in marker, or flip the card over and use the other side for the front.*)

8 Using crayons or colored markers, color the front of the card. You can draw in details for the shape you chose, or just do a design—whatever you think looks best.

9 Write your thank-you note on the inside of the card.

Potato-Stamp Card

IMPORTANT NOTE   This activity uses either stamp-pad ink or poster paints. If you're going to use ink from a stamp pad, you need to carve the potato and let it dry at least 24 hours in advance, so it will pick up the ink. (This step is not necessary if you use poster paints.)

MATERIALS NEEDED   One piece of reasonably heavy paper (computer paper or construction paper, or even light card stock); scrap paper; a potato; a sharp knife **(to be used by an adult!)**; one or two stamp pads (each of a different color) OR poster paints; pen

PROCEDURE

1 Fold the piece of paper in half and turn it sideways so the fold is to your left. (It will now open like a standard greeting card.)

2 You are going to create one or two stamps (like a rubber stamp) out of the two halves of a potato. One good bet for a design is your first and/or last initial. You can also do simple shapes, such as a heart, star, triangle, or square. Have a parent or other responsible adult cut a potato in half (around the middle, not end to end), then carve it so your design juts out of the potato half. (**Hint:** *The adult should remember that letters need to be carved "backward" so they stamp correctly.*) If you want to stamp *both* your initials, have the adult cut your other initial out of the other half of the potato.

3 Now is the point where you get involved again. Holding the uncut end of the potato, press it down on a stamp pad or in some poster paint to pick up the color. Then press your stamp on the front of the card to imprint your design onto the paper. (Here's one case when it's perfectly fine to "play with your food"!) Rock the potato back and forth as you press firmly onto the card, to make sure the whole shape stamps—your potato might have uneven surfaces!

4 You can stamp just one time or several times, depending on the look you want and on how large the potato stamp is. If it takes up close to half the card, stamping it once in the middle is enough. (But you will surely be creating more than one card, so don't worry—you'll get more chances to stamp.) If the stamp is small, you can stamp your initial once in each corner, or create a circle of "B"s or "L"s—whatever your initial is. Or, if you chose a shape, you can stamp it all over the place!

5 You may want to use more than one color. If so, stamp on the piece of scrap paper till the color you were using has faded; then re-ink the potato stamp in the new color and proceed in the way that's described above.

6 Write your thank-you note on the inside of the card.

Stencil & Splatter Card

MATERIALS NEEDED   One piece of reasonably heavy paper (computer paper or construction paper, or even light card stock); one piece of heavy card stock such as cardboard or an old file folder; water-based paint or poster paint (you may have to add water if you use poster paint, to make splattering easier); paintbrush (a wide one with lots of firm bristles, or even a toothbrush, will work well); scissors; pen; newspaper to work on

PROCEDURE

1 Spread the newspaper out over your work surface.

2 Fold the piece of paper in half and turn it sideways so the fold is to your left. (It will now open like a standard greeting card.)

3 Cut out a piece of the heavy card stock or file folder, the same size as the front of your card. You will use this for your stencil.

4 Draw your initial or a simple shape (such as a tree, heart, star, boat, etc.) on the heavy card stock which you cut out in step 3.

5 Cut your initial or shape out from the card stock. You now have a stencil!

47

6 Lay the card down so that the front is facing up and in the right direction. Then lay the stencil you've made onto the front of the card.

7 Dip the paintbrush in the paint. Flick the paint lightly at the front of the card (or use your finger to help splatter it) so the paint spatters across the stencil and the front of the card. Repeat till there is plenty of paint on the front of the card (*don't move or touch the cut-out stencil*).

8 Wash out the paintbrush and dry it.

9 Using a different color paint, repeat step 7.

10 Two colors of paint are probably enough, but if you want to use more than two colors, repeat steps 8 and 9.

11 Write your thank-you note on the inside of the card.